Harry Swotter

A HARRY POTTER QUIZ BOOK

RICH JEPSON

UNOFFICIAL & UNAUTHORIZED

QUIZ BOOKS BY RICH JEPSON

MOVIES

- Harry Swotter: A Harry Potter Quiz Book
- Monsters, Think.: A Pixar Movies Quiz Book
- Quizino Royale: A James Bond Quiz Book
- Riddle Earth: A Lord of the Rings Quiz Book
- TriviAvengers Assemble: A Marvel Cinematic Universe Quiz Book
- Risky Quizness: An 80s Movies Quiz Book
- Edward Quizorhands: A 90s Movies Quiz Book
- Quiztrict 9: A 2000s Movies Quiz Book
- Never Been Quizzed: A Romantic Comedies Quiz Book

TV

- Brain Of Thrones: A Game of Thrones Quiz Book
- Examinate: A Doctor Who Quiz Book
- Mental Perk: A Friends Quiz Book
- Quiz My Face: An Alan Partridge Quiz Book
- The Walking Egghead: A Walking Dead Quiz Book
- Wisenberg: A Breaking Bad Quiz Book

HARRY SWOTTER: A HARRY POTTER QUIZ BOOK

This edition published 2021

ISBN: 9781549697135

INTRODUCTION

In 1990, J.K. Rowling' was travelling from Manchester to London's King Cross when her train experienced a delay. She passed the time by devising a story about a young boy who discovered he was a wizard.

Fast-forward a few decades, and that young wizard has become one of the most iconic characters in literary and cinematic history.

The Harry Potter book series has sold over 450 million copies worldwide, receiving numerous awards and accolades along the way. These iconic novels have charmed the hearts of millions of fans of all ages across the globe, and it's these books that spawned the Harry Potter film series – and that's where this book comes in.

Inside this book, you will find 400 questions designed to test your knowledge of the Harry Potter films. Questions become increasingly difficult as you advance through the book.

There are fifteen general knowledge rounds and ten based on specific subjects or themes, including a quiz on *Fantastic Beasts And Where to Find Them*.

There's also a round of jokes and tiebreakers designed to help you figure out who knows the most about Harry Potter and J.K Rowling's Wizarding World.

Will you score 10 points for Gryffindor, or will you Slytherin to last place? Either way, you should never forget...

Yer a quizzard, Harry!

CONTENTS

QUESTIONS

QUIZ 1 - GENERAL KNOWLEDGE

1   Which actor plays Harry Potter?

2   Where does Hagrid take Harry to buy his school supplies?

3   What is the name of Harry's owl?

4   What shape does Harry's Patronus take?

5   Where in their house did the Dursleys make Harry sleep when he was a child?

6   Which platform does the Hogwarts Express run from at London King's Cross station?

7   What is the name of Harry's cousin?

8   What was Harry's first broomstick?

9   What is the name of the wizarding world's newspaper?

10 Where does the Dursley family live?

11 Harry is placed in which schoolhouse?

12 Who teaches potions at Hogwarts?

13 What shape is Harry's scar?

14 What object is Professor Slughorn disguised as when Harry first meets him?

15 Who is the 'Prisoner of Azkaban'?

Answers - Page 68

QUIZ 2 - GENERAL KNOWLEDGE

1   Where do Harry and Cho share their first kiss?

2   What creatures guard Azkaban?

3   What is the name of Dumbledore's phoenix?

4   What was the name of Ron's pet rat?

5   What did the Boggart turn into when Parvati Patil faced it?

6   Civilians outside of the Wizarding World are known by what nickname?

7   Who is the caretaker at Hogwarts?

8   How did the Dursleys explain the death of Harry's parents to him?

9   What is the name of Fred and George's joke shop?

10 What is the name of the journalist who interviews Harry during the Triwizard Tournament?

11 Which character does Emma Watson play?

12 What are Hagrid's students told they must do when approaching a Hippogriff?

13 In *Deathly Hallows: Part 1*, Voldemort and his forces are deceived by how many Decoy Harrys?

14 Who is the 'Half-Blood Prince'?

15 How do members of the wizarding community send their mail?

Answers - Page 69

QUIZ 3 - GENERAL KNOWLEDGE

1   What is the name of the portrait that guards the entrance to Gryffindor Tower?

2   What vehicle picks up Harry at the start of the Prisoner of Azkaban?

3   What initials does Harry find written on a piece of paper inside the fake locket?

4   What does Hagrid do to Dudley during his first visit to the Dursleys?

5   What subject does Professor McGonagall teach?

6   Which character does Rupert Grint play?

7   What object does Draco Malfoy first try to send through the vanishing cabinet?

8   What is the name of Hermione's cat?

9   What is the name of the network that wizards use to travel
between fireplaces?

10 What was the name of the Hagrid's three-headed dog?

11 How many Weasley children are there?

12 What object does Hermione use to attend multiple classes at
the same time?

13 What was the name of the House-elf who served the House
of Black?

14 What colour is the Slytherin coat of arms?

15 Who discovers Harry injured, beneath his invisibility cloak,
on the Hogwarts Express?

Answers - Page 70

QUIZ 4 – GENERAL KNOWLEDGE

1 Who is Harry's godfather?

2 What false name does Harry give the staff of the Knight Bus?

3 Who was Hermione's date for the Yule Ball?

4 Inside the house where Horace Slughorn was staying, what type of blood dripped from the ceiling?

5 What does Lupin give to Harry to make him feel better after the dementor attack on the Hogwarts Express?

6 How many years have passed between the battle of Hogwarts and the final scene of Deathly Hallows Part 2?

7 Who is the Charms teacher at Hogwarts?

8 Which chess piece did Ron replace in the chessboard chamber?

9   Which character died whilst Harry was being transported from Privet Drive to The Burrow?

10 What's the name of the hippogriff that injures Malfoy during the care of magical creatures' class?

11 Where did Harry's parents live?

12 Where do Harry and Ginny hide the Half-Blood Prince's potions book?

13 Who was the first person to get sorted into a Hogwarts house?

14 Which actor plays Professor Severus Snape?

15 Who bought Hedwig for Harry?

Answers - Page 71

QUIZ 5 - GENERAL KNOWLEDGE

1   Who finds the Room of Requirement for Dumbledore's Army?

2   Which actor plays Rubeus Hagrid?

3   How old is Harry when he finds out that he is a wizard?

4   Whose memory shows a young Tom Riddle at an orphanage?

5   Who built the Chamber of Secrets?

6   What does Bellatrix insist that Snape make with Narcissa Malfoy?

7   What is the name of Hagrid's Acromantula, which Harry and Ron encounter in the Forbidden Forest?

8   What item did Harry receive from Dumbledore in his will?

9   Who sent Harry a Firebolt broomstick in The Prisoner of Azkaban?

10 Who told Umbridge how to enter the Room of Requirement?

11 Where is the Slytherin Common Room located?

12 What type of dragon does Harry fight in the first task of the Triwizard Tournament?

13 What flavour of 'Bertie Bott's Every Flavour Bean' did Dumbledore, unfortunately, eat when he was young?

14 Shortly before Sirius is killed, what name does he call Harry by mistake?

15 What does Harry want to be after he graduates from Hogwarts?

Answers - Page 72

QUIZ 6 – SCHOOLHOUSES

Name the schoolhouse that each of the following characters belongs to:

1   Luna Lovegood

2   Tom Riddle

3   Moaning Myrtle

4   Cedric Diggory

5   Gregory Goyle

6   Padma Patil

7   Parvati Patil

8   Zach Smith

9   Sirius Black

10 Severus Snape

11 Seamus Finnigan

12 Justin Finch-Fletchley

13 Regulus Black

14 Ginny Weasley

15 Cho Chang

16 Gilderoy Lockhart

17 Albus Dumbledore

18 Dolores Umbridge

19 Peter Pettigrew

20 Minerva McGonagall

Answers - Page 73

QUIZ 7 - QUIDDITCH

1   How many players are there on each Quidditch team?

2   How many points does a team receive for a goal?

3   What are the three kinds of balls used in Quidditch?

4   How many goal hoops does a keeper defend?

5   What shape are Quidditch pitches typically?

6   Who won the Quidditch World Cup in *The Goblet of Fire*?

7   Which team does Gwenog Jones represent?

8   How many points does a team receive for catching the golden snitch?

9   What position does Draco Malfoy play?

10 Viktor Krum plays Quidditch professionally for which country?

11 How long is a Quidditch pitch?

12 Which Quidditch position does Ron play?

13 Who is the Hogwarts Quidditch referee?

14 What is the name of the broom the Slytherin team all ride in *The Chamber of Secrets*?

15 Who is the Gryffindor team captain when Harry joins the team?

Answers - Page 74

QUIZ 8 – HE WHO MUST NOT BE NAMED

1   Voldermort grew up in an orphanage in which city?

2   What is Voldemort's real name?

3   What are the members of Voldemort's army called?

4   What subject did Voldemort want to teach at Hogwarts?

5   Which Hogwarts professor came to the orphanage to tell Voldemort he was a wizard?

6   Which house was Voldemort in at Hogwarts?

7   Who did Voldemort blame for opening the Chamber of Secrets?

8   What was Voldemort's blood status?

9   Who helped restore Voldemort to his body?

10 Who was Voldemort's favourite teacher at school?

11 When the Chamber of Secrets was first opened, who died as a result?

12 What does Voldemort take from Dumbledore's tomb?

13 Where does Voldemort say Harry must give himself up in *Deathly Hallows Part 2*?

14 Which actor played Lord Voldemort in Harry's first year?

15 What was Voldemort's mother called?

Answers - Page 75

QUIZ 9 – PATRONUS

Name the animal form of each of the following characters' Patronus:

1 Ron Weasley

2 Ginny Weasley

3 James Potter

4 Albus Dumbledore

5 Cho Chang

6 Hermione Granger

7 Seamus Finnigan

8 Minerva McGonagall

9 Severus Snape

10 Arthur Weasley

11 Dolores Umbridge

12 Luna Lovegood

13 Kingsley Shacklebolt

14 Remus Lupin

15 Aberforth Dumbledore

16 Nymphadora Tonks

17 Rita Skeeter

18 Lily Potter

19 Ernie Macmillan

20 J.K. Rowling

Answers - Page 76

QUIZ 10 – FANTASTIC BEASTS AND WHERE TO FIND THEM

1   Which year is the film set in?

2   What is Newt Scamander's occupation?

3   What is the American word for muggle?

4   What is the name of the wizarding speakeasy Newt visits?

5   What does MACUS stand for?

6   Inside what department store does Newt Scamander find the oversized Occamy?

7   What creature helps Tina Goldstein escape death?

8   The shells of Occamy eggs contain what material?

9   Jacob Kowalski works in what kind of factory?

10 What is the name of Newt's Thunderbird?

11 Which house was Newt part of at Hogwarts?

12 Who directed the film?

13 What is the name of the creature that attempted to rob the Steen National Bank?

14 New Salam Philanthropic Society (NSPS) is also known by what name?

15 What kind of dessert does Queenie make for Jacob and Newt?

Answers - Page 77

QUIZ 11 – GENERAL KNOWLEDGE

1   Who is the Beauxbatons Academy's school champion?

2   What is the name of the pub where the three friends go for a Butterbeer?

3   Rita Skeeter can turn into what creature?

4   How do Harry and the others escape Gringotts after they take a Horcrux?

5   Which sweetshop does Harry invisibly enter in *the Prisoner of Azkaban*?

6   What sentence does Umbridge instruct Harry to write with a 'blood quill'?

7   Who gives Harry the Gillyweed for the second Triwizard challenge?

8 Which actress plays Minerva McGonagall?

9 What is the Diadem of Ravenclaw?

10 Who does Harry take to the Yule Ball?

11 What is the new motto for the Ministry of Magic after Voldemort's forces take it over?

12 Which three objects make up the Deathly Hallows?

13 Who helps Harry figure out what to do with the golden egg?

14 Who sets fire to The Burrow?

15 Which schoolhouse has a badger on its coat of arms?

Answers - Page 78

QUIZ 12 – GENERAL KNOWLEDGE

1 How do you open 'The Monster Book of Monsters'?

2 What does Harry use in the Headmaster's office to see Snape's memories?

3 What breed is Hagrid's pet Dragon?

4 What does Ron's mother send him after discovering he and Harry drove the flying car to Hogwarts?

5 Which schoolhouse's coat of arms is blue?

6 Why does Harry fall off his broomstick in the Quidditch game against Hufflepuff?

7 What word does Bellatrix Lestrange carve into Hermione's arm?

8 What item did Ron receive in Dumbledore's will?

9   Which actor provides the voice of Dobby?

10 Who disguised himself as 'Mad Eye' Moody in *The Goblet of Fire*?

11 What is the name of the map that shows every person's location within Hogwarts?

12 Which chess piece did Harry replace in the chessboard chamber?

13 Which character does Gary Oldman play?

14 Who supplied Harry with his first wand?

15 Who did Neville Longbottom take to the Yule Ball?

Answers - Page 79

QUIZ 13 – GENERAL KNOWLEDGE

1   Which actor plays Professor Filius Flitwick?

2   Who leads Harry, Ron and Hermione through the passageway to Hogwarts, shown to them by Aberforth?

3   What is the name of the Squib who witnesses the dementor attack on Harry and Dudley?

4   Which sweets created by the Weasley twins cause instant 'sickness'?

5   Where did the Snatchers take Harry, Ron and Hermione?

6   Who did Ron turn into when he and the others snuck into the Ministry of Magic?

7   Decoy Harrys are made using what potion?

8   Who is the House Ghost of Hufflepuff?

9 Who is the person that Ron beats to become Keeper for the Gryffindor Quidditch team?

10 What was the name of the student group set up by Dolores Umbridge to maintain order in Hogwarts?

11 When Bellatrix and Narcissa Malfoy visit Snape before the start of the school term, who do they find living with him?

12 What colour are Dobby's eyes?

13 The tunnel under the Whomping Willow leads where?

14 What did the Boggart turn into while facing Professor Lupin?

15 What did Ron use to destroy Slytherin's locket?

Answers - Page 80

QUIZ 14 - GENERAL KNOWLEDGE

1   What is the common name of the potion, 'Felix Felicis'?

2   What was the name of the book Hermione received in Dumbledore's will?

3   Who owns the flying motorcycle that Hagrid borrows to transport Harry to the Dursley house?

4   How far back in time does Tom Riddle's diary take Harry?

5   Who put Harry's name in the Goblet of Fire?

6   What does Harry give to Dobby to free him from his master?

7   Who serves drinks at Slughorn's party?

8   Where does Harry go when he uses the Marauder's Map for the first time?

9   Who takes over as Minister for Magic after the Death Eaters'
    coup?

10 What is Tonks first name?

11 Who is Sirius Black's father?

12 Who did Hermione take to Slughorn's Christmas party?

13 Who was the Hogwarts Professor of Muggle Studies?

14 Which actor plays Argus Filch?

15 What do Hermione's parents do for a living?

Answers - Page 81

QUIZ 15 – GENERAL KNOWLEDGE

1   What does O.W.L. stand for?

2   Who does Harry take to Slughorn's Christmas party?

3   Which spell saves Hermione from the troll?

4   What is Cedric Diggory's father's first name?

5   After escaping the wedding, which street do Harry, Ron and Hermione reappear on?

6   Who does Harry meet during his first visit to the Leaky Cauldron?

7   Who does Harry ask to help him break into Bellatrix Lestrange's vault at Gringotts bank?

8   What is the name of Hagrid's 16ft tall half-brother?

9   Which spell conjures up 'The Dark Mark' in the air?

10 What organisation did Hermione start in her 4th year?

11 Whilst in Bellatrix's vault, what does Harry discover the
    Horcrux is?

12 Which actress plays Luna Lovegood?

13 What's the first potion Harry brews thanks to the Half-Blood
    Prince's instructions perfectly?

14 What is the name of the French Wizarding school?

15 When is Harry's birthday?

Answers - Page 82

QUIZ 16 – CAST AND CREW

1   Who directed the first two Harry Potter films?

2   Which actor went on to become the 10th Doctor in the B.B.C. sci-fi drama *Doctor Who*?

3   Which actor played Arthur Kipps in the horror film, *The Woman in Black*?

4   Which two real-life twins played the roles of Fred & George Weasley?

5   Which Harry Potter actor also had a lead role in the *Twilight* series of films?

6   Which actress went on to star in *The Perks of Being a Wallflower* & *My Week with Marilyn*?

7   How old was actor Daniel Radcliffe when he began filming as Harry Potter?

8   Which actor also appeared in *The Patriot, Black Hawk Down* & *Peter Pan*?

9   What was the name of Alan Rickman's character in *Die Hard*?

10 How many Harry Potter films did David Yates direct?

11 Which Harry Potter actor also appeared in the B.B.C. comedy *Life's Too Short*?

12 When auditioning, which young Harry Potter actor submitted a tape showing them performing a rap they wrote for the role?

13 Which actress went on to play Violet Crawley in *Downton Abbey*?

14 In which city was Emma Watson born?

15 Which actor played the role of Valentin Zukovsky in two James Bond films?

Answers - Page 83

QUIZ 17 - SPELLS

What does each of the following spells and charms do?

1   Lumos (LOO-mos)

2   Oculus Reparo (ok-ul-lus re-pa-ro)

3   Alohomora (al-LOH-ha-MOHR-ah)

4   Riddikulus (rih-dih-KUL-lus)

5   Stupefy (STOO-puh-fye)

6   Sectumsempra (sec-tum-SEMP-rah)

7   Accio (AK-ee-oh)

8   Expecto Patronum (ecks-PECK-toh pah-TROH-numb)

9   Petrificus Totalus (pe-TRI-fi-cus to-TAH-lus)

10 Expelliarmus (ex-PELL-ee-ARE-muss)

11 Crucio (KROO-shea-oh)

12 Imperio (im-PEER-ee-oh)

13 Obliviate (oh-BLI-vee-ate)

14 Avada Kedavra (ah-VAH-dah keh-DAV-rah)

15 Wingardium Leviosa (win-GAR-dee-um lev-ee-OH-sa)

16 Bombarda Maxima (BOM-bar-dah MAX-ih-mah)

17 Diminuendo (dim-in-YEW-en-DOUGH)

18 Finestra (fi-NESS-tra)

19 Geminio (jeh-MIH-nee-oh)

20 Harmonia Nectere Passus (har-MOH-nee-a NECK-teh-ray
    PASS-us)

Answers - Page 84

QUIZ 18 - DEATHS

Name the person that was responsible for the death of each of the following characters:

1 Cedric Diggory

2 Sirius Black

3 Albus Dumbledore

4 Alastor Moody

5 Nagini

6 Lily & James Potter

7 Moaning Myrtle

8 Bathilda Bagshot

9 Dobby

10 Barty Crouch Snr

11 Bellatrix Lestrange

12 Severus Snape

13 Serpent of Slytherin

14 Scabior

15 Helena Ravenclaw

Answers - Page 85

QUIZ 19 - QUOTES

Name the characters that said each of the following quotes:

1   "Yer a wizard Harry"

2   "This boy will be famous. There won't be a child in our world who doesn't know his name."

3   "Come to me, let me rip you."

4   "Wit beyond measure is a man's greatest treasure."

5   "Odd sort of place, this, isn't it?"

6   "Do take care, won't you, Harry?"

7   "We had to use Neville instead!"

8   "Wow, we're identical!"

9   "Oh no, you don't, laddie!"

10 "And here comes Mr Krum!"

11 "We've all got both light and darkness inside us. What matters is the part we choose to act on. That's who we really are."

12 "We are only as strong as we are united, as weak as we are divided."

13 "Greatness inspires envy; envy engenders spite; spite spawns lies."

14 "It is the quality of one's convictions that determines success, not the number of followers."

15 "Kill the spare"

Answers - Page 86

QUIZ 20 - ANAGRAMS

Solve each of the following anagrams to reveal the name of a character:

1   I BRUSHED A RUG

2   OLD BULB MEASURED

3   PEN VERSUS SEA

4   MOVING TO TELL NOBLE

5   A LOGO UNLOVED

6   A SKI CLUB SIR

7   UNSURE LIMP

8   GAMING CAVEMAN ROLL

9   TROPHY RATER

10 OLD FOAMY CAR

11 THICK GALLERY DOOR

12 EMERGING HERO RAN

13 GREAT EXTERNAL BILLS

14 MOD REVOLT

15 ONES LAWYER

Answers - Page 87

QUIZ 21 – GENERAL KNOWLEDGE

1   Who was the Quidditch commentator in Harry's first year at Hogwarts?

2   Which creatures attack Harry and Dumbledore as they try to retrieve the locket?

3   Which spell does Draco Malfoy use on Harry when he's hiding in the luggage rack?

4   Which character is also known as Moony?

5   What was the name of the female elf Dobby liked?

6   When the snatchers catch the trio, what does Hermione say her name is?

7   What exam were the fifth year students taking when Fred and George disrupted it with a fireworks show?

8   Which actress plays Ginny Weasley?

9   What object do the students have to change their animals into during a lesson in Transfiguration?

10 What does R.A.B. stand for?

11 Who puts the love potion in the chocolates that Ron eats?

12 Which chess piece did Hermione replace in the chessboard chamber?

13 What breed of dragon did Fleur Delacour have to face during the Triwizard Tournament?

14 Which spell does Professor McGonagall cast to bring the suits of armour to life to protect the school?

15 Which four characters appear through the resurrection stone for Harry?

Answers - Page 88

QUIZ 22 - GENERAL KNOWLEDGE

1   Which bridge is destroyed by Death Eaters at the start of *The Half-Blood Prince*?

2   What happened to Neville's parents that resulted in them being unable to remember their son?

3   What is the name of the goblin that gets incinerated by the Ukrainian Ironbelly?

4   Where was the lost Diadem of Ravenclaw?

5   What potion did Harry take to get Slughorn's memories?

6   What time do Harry and Hermione travel back to so they can save Sirius and Buckbeak?

7   Who informed Harry, Ron and Hermione of the legacies left to them in Dumbledore's will?

8 How are the Death Eaters Amycus and Alecto Carrow related?

9 Which character does Emma Thompson play?

10 What subject does Harry study in private with Professor Snape to help him block out his nightmares?

11 What is the primary use of a Mandrake?

12 What shop on Knockturn Alley specialises in antiques related to the Dark Arts?

13 Where did Dobby transport Harry and the others to during their escape from Malfoy Manor?

14 What item did Griphook hold in his hand as he died?

15 What is the name of the Centaur who saves Harry from Voldemort in the Forbidden Forest?

Answers - Page 89

QUIZ 23 – GENERAL KNOWLEDGE

1   How did Harry survive underwater in the Triwizard Tournament?

2   Which character does Mark Williams play?

3   Who nearly dies after touching a cursed necklace?

4   How many presents did Dudley initially get on his birthday before screaming for more?

5   What is the name of Marjorie Dursley's dog?

6   Where is the order of the Phoenix headquarters located?

7   What is the name of the Scandinavian wizarding school?

8   How much did Harry's wand cost?

9   Who took Fleur Delacour to the Yule Ball?

10 What is the name of the Executioner appointed by the Ministry of Magic to dispose of Buckbeak?

11 What is Professor Dumbledore's full name?

12 What is the make and model of the Weasley's flying car?

13 What magazine does Luna's father publish?

14 What phrase does the golden snitch reveal after Harry presses it to his lips?

15 Who does Ron Weasley kiss in the Ministry of Magic?

Answers - Page 90

QUIZ 24 - GENERAL KNOWLEDGE

1   Who is the Conductor of the Knight Bus?

2   Which creatures attack Fleur Delacour in the second task of the Triwizard Tournament?

3   Who sends Harry his letter of expulsion from Hogwarts?

4   The Dursleys claimed they sent Harry to which school?

5   What colour is the feather of Rita Skeeter's quill when she interviews Harry?

6   Who is the Headmaster of the Durmstrang Institute?

7   What does Harry give Ron as an antidote after Ron drinks the poisoned mead?

8   Sirius was wrongly imprisoned for multiple counts of murder. How many?

9   What is Harry's youngest son's name?

10   What phrase appears on Dobby's tombstone?

11   Which actor plays Draco Malfoy?

12   What colour frosting is on Harry's birthday cake from Hagrid?

13   What's the name of James Potter's animagus stag?

14   What spell did Harry perform on Draco Malfoy during their fight in the bathroom?

15   Who wrote an obituary for Dumbledore in the Daily Prophet?

Answers - Page 91

QUIZ 25 – GENERAL KNOWLEDGE

1   Who was the Care of Magical Creatures Professor before Hagrid?

2   Who does Hermione take a hair from for the Polyjuice Potion, which accidentally turned out to be cat hair?

3   What is Gilderoy Lockhart's favourite colour?

4   What is Nearly Headless Nick's real name?

5   What is at the core of Lucius Malfoy's wand?

6   What is the English translation of the Hogwarts motto?

7   What is the name of the fish Lily Potter gave Professor Slughorn when she was a student?

8   Which actor plays Neville Longbottom?

9 What page does Snape ask them to turn to while covering for Lupin's class?

10 What does Professor Vector teach?

11 What is the name of the landlady of the Three Broomsticks pub?

12 Where does Dudley Dursley attend school?

13 What plant did Neville Longbottom get for his birthday?

14 Who was Headmaster of Hogwarts when Tom Riddle was at school?

15 What is the last word Harry speaks in the entire film series?

Answers - Page 92

TIEBREAKERS

1   How much, in British pounds, did the first Harry Potter film take?

2   How much, in U.S. dollars, did it cost to create the Wizarding World of Harry Potter theme park in Florida?

3   How many copies were there of the initial print run for Harry Potter and the Philosopher's Stone?

4   During the filming of the Whomping Willow crash scene, multiple Ford Anglias were destroyed. How many?

5   How many different products are there in the Weasleys' Wizard Wheezes Shop?

6   How many times did the make-up team apply Harry Potter's famous scar throughout the whole series?

7   How many copies of *Harry Potter and The Deathly Hallows* sold on the first day of sales?

8   How long would it take to watch the entire series of films back-to-back?

9   The Harry Potter books have been published in how many languages (to date)?

10 How much were the average earnings of each Harry Potter film in U.S. dollars?

Answers - Page 93

ANSWERS

QUIZ 1 - ANSWERS

1 Daniel Radcliffe

2 Diagon Alley

3 Hedwig

4 A stag

5 In the cupboard under the stairs

6 9 3/4

7 Dudley

8 Nimbus 2000

9 The Daily Prophet

10 4 Privet Drive

11 Gryffindor

12 Professor Snape

13 Lightning Bolt

14 An armchair

15 Sirius Black

QUIZ 2 - ANSWERS

1. In the Room of Requirement
2. Dementors
3. Fawkes
4. Scabbers
5. A snake
6. Muggles
7. Argus Filch
8. They said his parents died in a car crash
9. Weasleys' Wizard Wheezes
10. Rita Skeeter
11. Hermione Grainger
12. Bow
13. 6
14. Severus Snape
15. By Owl

QUIZ 3 - ANSWERS

1. The Fat Lady
2. The Knight Bus
3. R.A.B.
4. He gives him a pig's tail
5. Transfiguration
6. Ron Weasley
7. An apple
8. Crookshanks
9. The Floo Network
10. Fluffy
11. 7
12. A time turner
13. Kreacher
14. Green
15. Luna Lovegood

QUIZ 4 - ANSWERS

1. Sirius Black
2. Neville Longbottom
3. Viktor Krum
4. Dragon's blood
5. Chocolate
6. 19 years
7. Professor Filius Flitwick
8. A knight
9. Alastor "Mad-Eye" Moody
10. Buckbeak
11. Godric's Hollow
12. The Room of Requirement
13. Hermione Granger
14. Alan Rickman
15. Rubeus Hagrid

QUIZ 5 - ANSWERS

1. Neville Longbottom
2. Robbie Coltrane
3. 11
4. Albus Dumbledore
5. Salazar Slytherin
6. The Unbreakable Vow
7. Aragog
8. A golden snitch
9. Sirius Black
10. Cho
11. In the dungeons, under the lake
12. Hungarian Horntail
13. Vomit
14. James
15. An Auror

QUIZ 6 - ANSWERS

1. Ravenclaw
2. Slytherin
3. Ravenclaw
4. Hufflepuff
5. Slytherin
6. Ravenclaw
7. Gryffindor
8. Hufflepuff
9. Gryffindor
10. Slytherin
11. Gryffindor
12. Hufflepuff
13. Slytherin
14. Gryffindor
15. Ravenclaw
16. Ravenclaw
17. Gryffindor
18. Slytherin
19. Gryffindor
20. Gryffindor

QUIZ 7 - ANSWERS

1. 7
2. 10 points
3. Quaffle, Bludger & Golden Snitch
4. 3
5. Oval
6. Ireland
7. Holyhead Harpies
8. 150 points
9. Seeker
10. Bulgaria
11. 500ft
12. Keeper
13. Rolanda Hooch
14. Nimbus 2001
15. Oliver Wood

QUIZ 8 - ANSWERS

1. London

2. Tom Marvolo Riddle

3. Death Eaters

4. Defence Against the Dark Arts

5. Dumbledore

6. Slytherin

7. Hagrid

8. Half-Blood

9. Peter Pettigrew

10. Professor Horace Slughorn

11. Moaning Myrtle Warren

12. The Elder Wand

13. The Forbidden Forest

14. Richard Bremmer

15. Merope Riddle (née Gaunt)

QUIZ 9 - ANSWERS

1. Jack Russell Terrier
2. Horse
3. Stag
4. Phoenix
5. Swan
6. Otter
7. Fox
8. Tabby Cat
9. Doe
10. Weasel
11. Persian Cat
12. Hare
13. Lynx
14. Wolf
15. Goat
16. Wolf
17. Beetle
18. Doe
19. Boar
20. Herron

QUIZ 10 – ANSWERS

1. 1926
2. Magizoologist
3. No-Maj
4. The Blind Pig
5. Magical Congress of the United States of America
6. Macy's
7. Swooping Evil
8. Silver
9. Canning
10. Frank
11. Hufflepuff
12. David Yates
13. Niffler
14. Second Salemers
15. A Strudel

QUIZ 11 - ANSWERS

1. Fleur Delacour

2. The Three Broomsticks

3. A beetle

4. On the back of a dragon

5. Honeydukes

6. "I must not tell lies."

7. Neville Longbottom

8. Maggie Smith

9. A tiara

10. Parvati Patil

11. Magic is Might

12. The Elder Wand, the Resurrection Stone and the Cloak of Invisibility

13. Cedric Diggory

14. Bellatrix Lestrange

15. Hufflepuff

QUIZ 12 - ANSWERS

1. You stroke it down the spine
2. Pensieve
3. Norwegian Ridgeback
4. A howler
5. Ravenclaw
6. Because he sees a hoard of Dementors
7. Mudblood
8. His deluminator
9. Toby Jones
10. Barty Crouch, Jr.
11. Marauder's Map
12. A bishop
13. Sirius Black
14. Garrick Ollivander
15. Ginny Weasley

QUIZ 13 - ANSWERS

1. Warwick Davis
2. Neville Longbottom
3. Mrs Frigg
4. Puking Pastilles
5. Malfoy Manor
6. Reginald Cattermole
7. Polyjuice
8. Fat Friar
9. Cormac McLaggen
10. The Inquisitorial Squad
11. Peter Pettigrew (Wormtail)
12. Green
13. The Shrieking Shack
14. A full moon
15. The Sword of Gryffindor

QUIZ 14 – ANSWERS

1. Liquid Luck

2. The Tales of Beedle the Bard

3. Sirius Black

4. 50 years

5. Barty Crouch Jr. (disguised as Alastor Moody)

6. A sock

7. Neville Longbottom

8. Hogsmeade

9. Pius Thicknesse

10. Nymphadora

11. Orion Black

12. Cormac McLaggen

13. Charity Burbage

14. David Bradley

15. They are both dentists

QUIZ 15 - ANSWERS

1. Ordinary Wizarding Level
2. Luna Lovegood
3. Wingardium Leviosa
4. Amos
5. Tottenham Court Road
6. Professor Quirrel
7. Griphook
8. Grawp
9. Morsmordre
10. Society for the Promotion of Elfish Welfare (SPEW)
11. Helga Hufflepuff's cup
12. Evanna Lynch
13. The Draught of Living Death
14. Beauxbatons Academy of Magic
15. 31st July (the same as J.K Rowling)

QUIZ 16 - ANSWERS

1. Chris Columbus
2. David Tennant
3. Daniel Radcliffe
4. James & Oliver Phelps
5. Robert Pattinson
6. Emma Watson
7. 11
8. Jason Isaacs
9. Hans Gruber
10. 4
11. Warwick Davis
12. Rupert Grint
13. Maggie Smith
14. Paris, France
15. Robbie Coltrane

QUIZ 17 - ANSWERS

1. Turns the tip of the wand into a torch
2. Repairs eyeglasses
3. Used to open and unlock doors
4. Transforms Boggarts into something silly
5. Stuns victim
6. Creates prominent, blood-oozing gashes on the subject
7. Summons an object to the caster
8. Conjures a protective spirit-like incarnation
9. Temporarily binds the victim's body
10. It causes whatever the victim is holding to fly away
11. Inflicts intense pain on the recipient of the curse
12. Places the subject in a dream-like state, in which they are utterly subject to the will of the caster
13. Used to hide a memory of a particular event
14. Causes instant death to the victim
15. Levitates moves and manipulates the target
16. Creates a large explosion capable of removing entire walls
17. It causes the target to shrink in size
18. Forces glass to shatter
19. Duplicates the target
20. Repairs a Vanishing Cabinet

QUIZ 18 – ANSWERS

1. Peter Pettigrew (as per Lord Voldemort's orders)

2. Bellatrix Lestrange

3. Severus Snape (secretly under Albus' orders)

4. Lord Voldemort

5. Neville Longbottom

6. Lord Voldemort

7. Salazar Slytherin's Basilisk

8. Nagini

9. Bellatrix Lestrange

10. Barty Crouch Jr (posing as Alastor Moody)

11. Molly Weasley

12. Nagini

13. Harry Potter

14. Neville Longbottom

15. Bloody Baron

QUIZ 19 – ANSWERS

1. Rubeus Hagrid
2. Professor McGonagall
3. The Basilisk
4. Luna Lovegood
5. Gilderoy Lockhart
6. Molly Weasley
7. Oliver Wood
8. Fred and George Weasley
9. Mad-Eye Moody
10. Mr Bagman
11. Sirius Black
12. Albus Dumbledore
13. Tom Riddle
14. Remus Lupin
15. Lord Voldemort

QUIZ 20 - ANSWERS

1. Rubeus Hagrid
2. Albus Dumbledore
3. Severus Snape
4. Neville Longbottom
5. Luna Lovegood
6. Sirius Black
7. Remus Lupin
8. Minerva McGonagall
9. Harry Potter
10. Draco Malfoy
11. Gilderoy Lockhart
12. Hermione Granger
13. Bellatrix Lestrange
14. Voldemort
15. Ron Weasley

QUIZ 21 - ANSWERS

1. Lee Jordan

2. Inferi

3. Petrificus Totalus

4. Remus Lupin

5. Winky

6. Penelope Clearwater

7. Potions

8. Bonnie Wright

9. Water goblets

10. Regulus Arcturus Black

11. Romilda Vane

12. Rook/Castle (Queen-side)

13. Common Welsh Green

14. Piertotum Locomotor

15. James Potter, Lily Potter, Sirius Black & Remus Lupin

QUIZ 22 - ANSWERS

1. Millennium Bridge

2. The Death Eaters used the Cruciatus Curse on them

3. Bogrod

4. In the Room of Requirement

5. Felix Felicis

6. 7.30 pm (3 hours prior)

7. Rufus Scrimgeour

8. Siblings

9. Professor Sybil Trelawney

10. Occlumency

11. To restore those who have been Petrified

12. Borgin and Burkes

13. Shell Cottage

14. Godric Gryffindor's Sword

15. Firenze

QUIZ 23 – ANSWERS

1. Gillyweed
2. Arthur Weasley
3. Katie Bell
4. 36
5. Ripper
6. 12 Grimmauld Place, London
7. Durmstrang Institute
8. Seven galleons
9. Roger Davies
10. MacNair
11. Professor Albus Percival Wulfric Brian Dumbledore
12. Ford Anglia (105E Deluxe)
13. The Quibbler
14. "I open at the close"
15. Mary Cattermole

QUIZ 24 - ANSWERS

1. Stan Shunpike

2. Grindylow

3. Mafalda Hopkirk

4. St. Brutus' Secure Centre
   for Incurably Criminal
   Boys

5. Green

6. Igor Karkaroff

7. A Bezoar

8. 13

9. Albus Severus Potter

10. "Here Lies Dobby, a Free
    Elf"

11. Tom Fellon

12. Pink (with green
    writing)

13. Prongs

14. Sectumsempra spell

15. Elphias Doge

QUIZ 25 – ANSWERS

1. Professor Kettleburn
2. Millicent Bulstrode
3. Lilac
4. Sir Nicholas de Mimsy-Porpington
5. Dragon Heartstring
6. "Never Tickle a Sleeping Dragon"
7. Francis
8. Matthew Lewis
9. 394
10. Arithmancy
11. Madame Rosmerta
12. Smeltings Academy
13. Mimbulus Mimbletonia
14. Armando Dippit
15. "Ready?"

TIEBREAKERS - ANSWERS

1. £604million

2. $200million

3. 1000

4. 14

5. 120

6. 5,800

7. 11million

8. 19.6hours

9. 79

10. $963,268,497

JOKES

1. Why does Voldemort only use Twitter and not Facebook?

2. Why was Harry Potter sent to the Headmaster's office?

3. How do Death Eaters freshen their breath?

4. Where can you find Dumbledore's Army?

5. Why is Mad-Eye Moody such a lousy teacher?

6. How does Harry Potter get rid of a rash?

7. What do you call a postal carrier that can speak to packages?

8. Why doesn't Voldemort have glasses?

9. What do you call the entrance to a magical gym?

10. What kind of cereal do they serve at Hogwarts?

11. Why did Snape stand in the middle of the road?

12. Why did Harry Potter throw away all his old potions?

13. How does Voldemort enter a room?

14. Why can't Harry Potter tell his potions pot and his best

    friend apart?

15. What do you call two Quidditch players who share a dorm?

16. What did Harry call his pet horse?

17. What do you call an electrocuted Dark Lord?

18. Why did Barty Crouch Jr. quit drinking?

19. What happens when Harry Potter says accidental?

20. What is bigfoot's favourite book?

Answers - Page 96

JOKES (ANSWERS)

1. Because he has followers and not friends

2. Because he was cursing in class

3. Dementos

4. Up his sleeve-y!

5. Because he can't control his pupils

6. With quit-itch

7. A parcel tongue

8. Nobody nose

9. A Dumbbell door

10. Huffle Puffs

11. So you'll never know which side he's on

12. They were past their hexpiration date

13. He slithers in

14. Because they're both cauld-ron

15. Broom-mates

16. Harry Trotter

17. Volt-demort!

18. Because it was making him Moody

19. Someone loses a tooth.

20. Hairy Potter

NOTES

Printed in Great Britain
by Amazon